THE ART OF THE THRIFT

PATRICK SPYCHALSKI

Table of Contents

To Everyone I've Met in a Thrift Store;
Thanks for the Memories.

THE THRIFT MANIFESTO

In my young, uninvited, yet outspoken opinion, the thrift store is one of the greatest business and humanitarian inventions of the last century. It's an adventure, an experience; in no other place can an unsuspecting shopper enter a store and have absolutely zero idea what is to be found behind the ever-so-welcoming door that precedes them. It's inevitably exciting items that one can't even think to be found in a normal retail setting is what sets apart the thrift store from any other subcategory of shopping experience, hands down. Of course, I'm biased, but it doesn't mean I'm not right. I've personally been the perfectly happy victim of a thrift store addiction for more than two years now, going to multiple locations a day if time allows- and trust me, it always will. My eyes constantly light up at the prospect that I'm able to waltz into a store that I was shopping in not 24 hours ago and find completely different items than in my previous trip. It's an adventure, one that costs about as much as a Big Mac and can be experienced in the everyday lives of people who couldn't otherwise feel a sense of excitement in their day.

This absolutely crazed outlook that many have on a grouping of assorted racks filled with used clothes shaded over by a dirty, unkempt structure is not without good reason, though. It's filled with bits and pieces of evidence from my own accounts, the tales of other resellers, and the healthy bank accounts of millions around the globe. Plain and simple, the thrift store is a monument to American retail culture, a staple of support to the less fortunate, and an infinitely expanding business opportunity to those brave and savvy enough to take advantage of it.

Before one delves themselves into the seemingly simple structure of the discount-chasing business model that thousands of entrepreneurs have followed for years, it is incredibly important to address the advantages of the thrift store; not just to the reseller, but to the average customer. More often than not, the self-made business men and women that constitute the thrift-flipping community started out as regular shoppers themselves, looking for anything ranging from a unique sense of style to a peculiarly-furnished household. It's these same shoppers that, whether it took a week or a year, realized the limitless economic benefits that can be achieved by applying an entrepreneurial viewpoint to the everyday life of a discount shopaholic. This trend proves to the utmost importance a main business point that can be seen in almost any industry- a great way to know what the customer wants is to first be one yourself.

The first advantage to indulging oneself to the world of thrift stores, an absolutely essential first that needs to be aforementioned to a lengthy list of pros that they provide us on a daily basis, is the prices. The main thing to know about these prices, although we're going to go a bit below the surface of the tag price, is the fact that unless you decide to rob a designer retailer or your Aunt Jennifer decides to gift a shirt to you for Christmas, the prices are absolutely unbeatable. This may seem like an opinion or a conditional statement, but a closer look at the economics of how many of these items are made provides a factual basis behind a claim as outlandish as this one. Think about it. A fashion brand such as Nike, Gucci, etc. won't even think for a second about pricing their items for below the price it took them to produce it. The costs of the fabric, machine time, packaging, and shipping alone add up to more than what a thrift store would put on its price tag, and this is without taking into account other expenses. Second-hand stores are the only place a firm has the ability to price an item at below the production costs and still turn a profit; this is due to the donations that thrift stores take in every day to restock their shelves. The thrift store model in itself is absolute genius, because the same people cover both the supply and demand side of the store. Customers drop off their own clothes in the donation center on the side of the storefront, and then trot through the doors of the same establishment and buy clothes right back, all without the store barely lifting a finger. This model, unless a massive technological change in the production of apparel comes out sometime in the near future, is basically the only way that someone could possibly grab a Louis Vuitton purse at a store, pay $4 to the employee working the register up front, and walk out of the store all without committing a crime. When I say the prices are unbeatable, I mean that they really are unbeatable.

These prices that I just hyped up a paragraph ago provide a pretty straightforward business advantage, as well- the profits can be insane. With a majority of thrift stores, the products are priced based off of their category, not from their individual value. For example, a Gucci shirt and a Walmart-brand shirt obviously have different values, but a thrift store sees them both at the core, simply pricing them as 'shirts'. A savvy businessman/woman can utilize their market knowledge in order to find some of the less obvious "Gucci vs Walmart" scenarios and reap huge profits.

Although this next benefit is definitely seen as more of an intangible, the adventure side of the thrift store experience is one that should never be discounted. It's the main reason I do it, and I'm the guy writing the book on thrifting which means you're getting an expert opinion right now. The thrift store is a miniature treasure hunt that can be embarked on every day, and tends to be within the comfort zone of a much larger population than a generic action movie-style treasure hunt would be. Most of the time, a shopper has to go through hundreds, if not thousands of assorted pieces of trash in order to find a true gem. For many, this can be seen as a pain, but for the right type of person (hopefully you), it makes it that much better. The sense of accomplishment when finding a great item on a rack can be just enough to motivate a person to go through dozens more just to find another one. It's an affordable, quick, repeatable, and possibly profitable adventure that can turn a hobby into a lifestyle and a lifestyle into a career. The best part about this adventure is that not everyone enjoys it, giving individuals who find pleasure in it a substantial advantage when attempting to turn thrifting into profit.

Italian scholar Francesco Petrarch once said "Sameness is the mother of disgust, variety is the cure". This quote summarizes the overall theme of the next point discussed better than I ever could, which is why I let Francesco take the intro. One characteristic that every store on Earth other than thrifts has is a theme. The sub-genres that most stores are categorized into are very helpful for the consumer, because the shopper can walk in and know what they expect to purchase; a designer clothing retailer is going to have designer clothes, a tire shop is going to have tires, and so on. The beautiful thing (or anxiety-causing thing, depends on what type of person you are) about thrifts is the insane variety that comes with a chaotic cluster of donated items scattered around shelves like a 4-year old organized it. It's like Walmart if the items were used, only had one in stock, and made no sense half the time. That's probably a discouraging analogy, but you can't say it isn't a bit intriguing as well. Variety is the reason people go in the first place; it's a one stop shop for quirky items that can't be found anywhere else.

From a business standpoint, variety is the only thing keeping us resellers in business; we are providing the service of digging through and creating organization out of the unorganized. If thrifts sold a fixed product, consumers would know exactly where to get it. McDonald's sells Big Macs, Sunglass Hut sells sunglasses, and thrift stores sell literally everything known to man but in a super unorganized way. The unknown is where resellers thrive, which is why taking advantage of variety is a key skill for every thrift enthusiast.

One day, while browsing the cluttered shelves of a thrift store in Costa Mesa, California, Teri Horton came across a massive, paint-splattered canvas that looked like a clinically insane man had taken a paintbrush and waved it around until the canvas was draped in colored streaks. She was an avid thrifter and made a living reselling trinkets and antiques that she has curated from her various thrifting sprees. Although she was in the store for business, she decided to buy the painting for $10 as a gag gift for her friend. She took wall-sized and paint-splattered canvas to her friend, who found it to have a striking resemblance to the works of legendary American abstract-expressionist painter Jackson Pollock. After taking it to multiple art experts Teri soon realized that her $10 gag gift was in fact an original work by the famed painter with a value of approximately $50 million.

I chose to tell this story, although it's obviously an outlier, because it emphasizes the possible rarity of many items found within the four walls of your local thrift establishment; many of the art, antiques, clothes, etc. found there are the same pieces being put up at auction with a 4-figure starting bid. It doesn't take a savvy art critic with an expertise in mid-century expressionist pieces to make these discoveries either. I was once in an Uber on the way to a thrift store outside of Philadelphia when the driver and I struck up a conversation about reselling. He told me that a month prior, he walked into the same thrift store that I was riding to after dropping a client off, just out of curiosity. He picked up an art print and, after some quick internet research, realized it was a print signed by 20th century surrealist artist Salvador Dali. He proceeded to resell it for almost a grand shortly after. That was my UBER DRIVER, folks. He wasn't running an art gallery, he wasn't attending weekly auctions, he was shuttling me around to a random thrift in Philly. Rare pieces like these aren't as uncommon as one may think, but they do require knowledge and persistence to find.

I would have absolutely loved to continue expressing my admiration of thrift stores for another hundred pages or so, but unfortunately, I must address the 'cons' of pulling up to thrift stores every day. Surprisingly this book isn't a text hyping up thrifts the whole time, and like all good things, they come with a couple downsides that should be acknowledged.

Something that you, prospective thrift connoisseur, must vitally understand about this profession is that it can often be incredibly time consuming. The time to drive to each and every thrift itself is relatively substantial, and this isn't even touching on the long hours it takes to sort through the thousands of items cluttering the shelves. Although thrifting has its shortcuts (literally the whole book is about this), it is still a time intensive occupation and one that requires a good bit of field work. I've had 12 hour thrift marathons that have wiped me out to my core, this statement coming from an avid long-distance runner whose primary responsibility every day is an eight to twelve mile run. Just like any worthwhile thing in life, it's a risk of one's limited and valuable time, energy, and thinking power.

Emphasis must also be put on whether a thrift is just having a natural and cyclical dry patch, or simply an inferior store to attend. The recommended determining visit number is around twenty; this meaning if you attend a particular thrift store twenty separate times and there is absolutely nothing even relatively tempting to purchase, then that thrift may simply have poor sourcing techniques or a less than ideal location. It is still definitely recommended that one visits every thrift in their area, but dealing with an inferior store may involve spacing out visits a bit more than other locations.

A secondary shortcoming that one may experience, a problem that ties in with the aforementioned time consumption complex, is the hit-or-miss nature of attending these diverse garage sale-like retail locations. If you want to make a living out of perusing the shelves of discount stores, you must have the utmost patience while doing so. There are days in which one walks into a thrift and there's a thousand dollars sitting on a rack, but there can also be times where there's literally nothing for weeks on end. I once had a 2-month dry period that pushed me to the very edge of hope for my local thrifts; I almost became the dreaded non-believer that I make my living selling to. I fell into a cycle involving walking into a thrift with zero confidence and walking out with even less, until I felt like I was crazy to even try anymore. A famous Einstein quote resonated in my head on a daily basis, "the definition of insanity is doing something over and over again and expecting a different result". I would think, *Does his quote apply to what I'm doing now? Did Einstein ever attend a thrift store?* and when things finally started to look positive in my local thrifts again, I said to myself, *that nerd definitely hasn't been to a Goodwill and probably doesn't even know what he's talking about.* At the end of the day, thrifting is <u>way</u> more complicated than space-time relativity and theoretical physics, so the best thing to do is stick to your undying faith in the thrifts and trust the process. Dry patches like these push one's patience to never before seen boundaries, but this adversity is also why the ones who stay resilient reap even larger rewards at the end.

One part of thrifting that can be advantageous to some, but awful to others is the 'loneliness' that tends to come with running around to thrifts all day. Unless you have a business partner or someone who is just as obsessed with thrifting as you are, you'll likely be spending long hours by yourself. Your 'coworkers' are generally either people who thrift as often as you or the members of the community in general. In other words, you'll make friends doing this, but you likely will not be able to take your childhood friends with you every day. I tend to see the time as an opportunity to reflect on other aspects of my life and to focus on the work ahead of me. Having people to come along with you can actually be detrimental to your productivity, even though it initially seems like a good idea. Tag-along friends will likely not want to spend 8 hours thrifting with you (could you imagine?) and will pressure you to get off your thrift grind. You really can't blame them; they're recreational thrifters that enjoy popping in and out of a store like it's a Gap. When doing this for REAL, that's usually not an option unless it's your third time in that thrift or something. Unless you're able to find a proper thrifting buddy, you'll have to prepare for some personal time.

Lastly, many (often entitled) people find thrift stores to be repulsive and of the lower class. Although this third point is categorized in the negatives section, I personally find it as a major advantage as well. I always feel a small sense of satisfaction when the naive bystander tries to criticize the way I make a living, mostly because their stuck-up ignorance is losing them heaps of money. I often try to preach the good word of thrifting to the people around me, and those who see themselves as 'above' thrifts are at a lifelong disadvantage. I won't lie though, there are certainly times where I've walked out of a thrift store and lathered every part of my body that touched something in hand sanitizer; they didn't earn that reputation for no reason. But, there is a significant difference in letting an obstacle slow you down as opposed to letting it completely deter you. The first time I walked into what is now my primary thrift of choice, I heard a squealing coming from one of the bins of shoes that the workers had just brought out. Upon further inspection, there had been a rat weaving in and out of the pairs of shoes inside the bin. One of the workers (who was definitely not being paid enough) threw on a pair of gloves, took the struggling rat out of the bin, and took it into the back room, never to be seen again. This scarring experience almost caused me to go home and cry in a bath full of hand sanitizer, but instead I nutted up and started combing through the shoes like nothing had happened. Shortly after, I scored a pair of Nike's worth a good bit of money. Every success comes with struggle.

I really wish I could say that all thrifts are created equally, but that simply isn't true. Some of them are spectacular, and some of them are hot garbage. It's the harsh reality of the game. What makes a thrift a good one is important to address because the sooner you're able to dismiss a rotten apple, the better.

The first (and honestly, most important) aspect of a good thrift is how often new items are brought out. This is the most important primarily because the odds of you walking out empty-handed are harshly cut as new items are displayed. My favorite thrifts are almost always the ones that make employees bring items out every ten minutes. The higher the thrift's inventory is, the better chance you have of scoring.

Of course, the quality of items is important as well. Some thrifts can just be absolute gold mines even though they don't have mountains of inventory. It's kind of like having a lanky friend who looks like they'd break just by attempting to pick up a weight, and then you show up at the gym and they can bench press twice your max. It's not likely to happen, but it does. The same concept applies to the smaller, mom-and-pop thrifts that you may come across. This is why you <u>never</u> dismiss a thrift simply because of its size. However, you can determine after a few trips whether the store is going to be worth your time by assessing the quality of the items there.

The third most important component of a good thrift (of course there's more, such as variety, vicinity, etc. but I don't want to be here all day) is how many people know about it. A thrift's secrecy isn't good for their business, but it's highly beneficial for yours. Thrifting is a million times easier when nobody knows about the store itself, because you don't necessarily have to rush as much. You would think that secrecy is kind of difficult with modern technology such as Google Maps, but there are a ton of thrifts that haven't established an internet presence at all. This makes them super hard to find. I have a couple thrifts in my area that almost <u>nobody</u> in my thrift circle knows about; they're on a random back road that nobody would ever think of checking. Usually, the only way to find these places is to stumble across them or to coax a friend into revealing the location. Anyway, these lowkey thrift stores can be super lucrative, even if they don't bring items out as often (which is generally the case). This is because no matter how amazing the items are in the thrift, nobody is going to buy them if nobody goes in there to begin with. To be honest, I have no clue how some of these thrifts remain in business, but I'm not complaining.

That was really the rant section of this book. I just had to get that out of the way because it's important to have passion when doing anything, and if you weren't even the least bit passionate during that short manifesto, then... change your mind. Things get more technical from this point on, mainly because this book, of course, has a purpose: to inform the reader on how to effectively make money by properly utilizing the thrifts.

Prefaces to an Empire

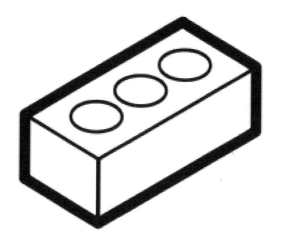

After just reading what was undoubtedly the most inspiring thrifting speech you've ever received, it's natural for someone to want to hop into whatever form of transportation they own and Tokyo drift themselves over to their nearest store. But YOU, the intelligent business person, want to build an empire, a name for yourself. Forming a defined plan about what your business will comprise of, who you will sell to, and where you will sell your product is the most efficient and cost-effective way to approach reselling. This section will outline and explain the different steps one must take in order to properly find a niche, a customer, and a platform to begin making the big boy/girl money.

The one commonality between any professional reseller is their ability to know almost everything about a particular product category; their deep-rooted specialization gives them an advantage to almost anyone entering a store. I know shoe people, book people, tech people, vintage people, toy people, and even people that literally just buy cowboy stuff. These people have found what is called a niche, a particular customer category that they are specifically targeting. As aforementioned in the previous chapter, our main job is creating organization out of the unorganized. A niche is a form of organization; we're taking products from an incredibly unorganized and confusing place and turning it into a consumer-friendly shopping experience. By taking advantage of the chaos within a thrift store, we can use our niche to gain a more dedicated following and a steadier income flow than somebody using the 'jack of all trades' method could. In general, a niche should be something you're particularly passionate or knowledgeable about. This will give you a significant advantage during the often tedious research that is required when attempting to achieve the "all-knowing master" level.

When a niche is finally chosen, the immediate next step is to conduct an absolutely ridiculous amount of research. I mean, like, a TON of research; to the point where you could go into the thrift without a phone and walk out knowing the exact value of the items in your hands. This is usually by far the most challenging part of planning out your reselling business, because it basically involves teaching yourself an entire micro-industry. In my case, I chose vintage men's clothes to be my niche. I already had a general knowledge of the culture and of the most popular money-making items, and I have always had a deep passion for the fashion industry in general. My bout of research involved a couple of hours per day of online window shopping, in which I would visit an assortment of sites and 'shop' for vintage clothes; I would see which styles, brands, and individual items went for the most money and take a mental note of it until an industry catalog was permanently lasered into my head.

A question that I know is probably in a couple of your heads when reading this section is, '*why on earth would someone EVER do that instead of just researching things as they go?'* To answer this question, I'll tell you a story. This isn't an experience of mine, but rather one of a colleague that thrifts primarily in northern Pennsylvania. A couple months prior to him telling me this story, he was sorting through a set of bins in a Goodwill Clearance that had just been brought out. He picked up a pair of ripped-up, dirty jeans and immediately dismissed them as trash, throwing them back in the strewn-about pile of clothes. A man walked up from behind him, eyeing the bin without touching anything until he swiftly picked up the pair of jeans that my friend had recently disposed of. He nonchalantly stated "These are worth a thousand dollars" and threw them in his cart. My friend later found out that these jeans were in his niche of vintage clothing, and he never even knew of their existence, much less their importance.

This story emphasizes two things: 1-Not every item in your niche will be obvious to point out, and 2-Nobody has time to look up thousands of individual items, just to find maybe a dozen that have significant value. This is why prior research is an absolutely vital preface to entering the doors of a thrift; these drastic research methods give a reseller confidence, as well as a priceless advantage in the long run. Entering any thrift and knowing that there are only a few, if any, possible people threatening your business is an amazing feeling, but is a feeling that requires work to be achieved.

An essential next step for any savvy business person when establishing their place in a specific niche is their brand. A brand name, logo, and presence is arguably the most important aspect of a company. What would McDonald's be without the arches? What would Louis Vuitton be without their iconic monogram logo? The branding is what makes or breaks a company, especially one that targets the individual purchaser. It adds to the consumer experience; if a customer has a positive transaction experience, your brand will be the first in mind when looking to purchase other items of the same niche. This is also the part of the business in which you, the reader, should have the most creativity. It's up to you to determine what sort of vibe you want to put off when advertising your business; of course, your name and logo will be one of the main influences of this. Do you want your company to be happy? Intense? Quirky? Sophisticated? Certain moods work better for certain niches. For example, if Hermés decided to give off a super-hip Hot Topic-like vibe, people probably wouldn't buy their bags for twenty thousand dollars. This is why picking your mood, brand name, and logo are imperative to creating later business success.

Networking is, and always will be, an instrumental part to any business; thrifting is no exception. The people that you surround yourself with have the ability to teach you more than books ever could (you should keep reading this one though). Locating, familiarizing yourself with, and personally meeting experts in your niche can make research significantly easier than trying it alone.

Don't make this thrifting endeavor harder than it is; utilize the people that worked for years to streamline their business and take their advice. These specialists likely have a plethora of experience in the same field you are attempting to pursue, which means they can tell you which aspects of the niche to avoid. I personally like to converse with individuals who specialize in thrifting in general, as well as people who specialize in my niche but do not thrift at all. I see it as a metaphorical Venn diagram in which thrifting and my niche are the two large circles that overlap, hence creating the smaller "both" section that comprises my business. It was initially incredibly difficult for me to finally admit to myself that I didn't actually know everything in the world and actually pursue networking opportunities, but I found the advantages to overwhelmingly outweigh the effort. Experimental business practices can often be a time consuming and costly activity, but simply asking those who have already tried similar endeavors can save priceless amounts of time.

With the internet's infinite development through the years, networking has been streamlined to the point where you can contact 3 people in a minute and have their responses before you've finished eating breakfast. Social media is, in my opinion, the most important and underutilized tool since the Shamwow. LinkedIn, Instagram, Facebook, carrier pigeon; the list goes on for ages. It blows my mind when someone tries to tell me that they cannot find help on a topic when they have access to BILLIONS of people from around the planet. A main issue with novice networking tactics is that people hop on their Instagram and message Elon Musk or something asking for marketing tactics; a key to properly finding mentors is creating attainable goals in terms of who you want to contact. There are plenty of incredibly intelligent people in every possible niche that may not have 100,000 Twitter followers, but have a wide array of knowledge that one can use to build their thrifting empire. As somebody with social anxiety, I often find it difficult to garner the courage to even try to bring about an inquiry to the array of experts I know. A great way to build this mental wall of courage is to tell yourself that you wouldn't have ever met this person to begin with, so asking them if you should 'light your clothes on fire to kill off the germs' probably won't affect your life very much. The point is, slide into those DM's. It'll literally pay off.

So, you've researched your niche. You've talked to people. You've finally gotten to the point where you feel as if you have an omnipotent grasp on the entirety of the subject you have been researching and you're ready to move on. So, what's next?

Often, who you're selling to is just as important as what you're selling. Selling hoverboards at a retirement home will likely not be as effective as eBay, and selling dentures to teenagers won't be too lucrative unless they enjoy chewing tobacco. An audience is usually talked about when discussing the definition of a niche (which we've already done), but what I'm specifically focusing on is whether your business wants to sell to businesses, or to the individual consumer. Figuring out what customer targeting method fits you best is an absolute key when determining the direction of your thrift business.

A B2C (Business to Consumer) strategy is what you think of when you think 'thrift reseller'; you sell straight to the consumer using the thousands of platforms available to do so. This strategy usually yields the most profit, and a hard-working B2C seller can build a brand relatively quickly. Think about it- just about every single brand you know is a B2C business. Starbucks, Walmart, Apple, etc. are all in the business of providing to the consumer and building their brand behind a quality service or product. This can result in a strong customer base and a steadier flow of income than if you were to rely on a single specific customer. For example, it would be incredibly difficult to impede on Starbucks' revenue stream because millions of people buy coffee from them a day. A huge problem would have to arise in order to contest their massive customer base.

However, B2C generally involves the most work due to the fact that one has to market each individual item in order to sell them. The often painstaking process of taking high-quality pictures, writing a detailed description of the item, pricing it, shipping it to the buyer, and performing customer service can be incredibly overwhelming. It's also super boring at times, making the work not only difficult but annoying to do as well. There have been countless times where

I've looked at a pile of clothes and internally groaned because I knew how much listing work was ahead of me. It's generally not something you can automate either, because each item usually has its own unique flaws, details, and features that need to be individually noted. Problems like these may also require you to eventually hire additional labor due to the time-intensive aspect of controlling the product's sales cycle. This can cause problems when the time comes around to scale your business, and the costs could be more than a beginner is able to handle.

A B2B (Business to Business) strategy is one that targets corporations as a whole, and generally involves less marketing than a B2C (Business to Consumer) strategy. When incorporating thrifting into the mix, many beginners have the question, '*how can I sell thrifted items to a business if they generally deal in standardized products?*' Actually, there are a wide array of brick-and-mortar businesses that act as a sort of indoor niche-run flea market, where they both buy and sell items specific to that niche (this could always be your strategy as well, if you have the funds to support it). Utilizing these businesses to your advantage and acting as a middleman is always an option when choosing a business structure.

Using myself as an example, I target stores that buy and sell clothing, usually vintage clothing. Round Two is a business that I sell to, one of their main niches being, you guessed it, vintage clothing. It is the most popular vintage clothing store in the world, with 4 separate retail locations around the world at the time of this book's publication. Sellers of all backgrounds enter their store with thrifted clothing, and Round Two pays them extremely fair amounts for the pieces they bring in. I love this idea for both parties because while Round Two benefits from gaining a bulletproof sourcing technique, the seller is able to get cash as fast as an ATM could give it to them. This is a great example of a store that B2B businesses can use to make a profit.

Many make a living by doing B2B because they don't have to spend any time taking pictures, listing, packaging, or shipping their clothes; they simply walk into the store with it and walk out with cash minutes later. Pawn shops, antique stores, and art auctioneers are all additional examples of B2B target destinations in which the seller has to do little to no work in order to get paid. Furthermore, a B2B buyer often purchases in bulk, and they buy almost anything as long as it follows their niche guidelines. Research is usually as simple as asking the store owner/manager what they are currently looking for and adhering to those guidelines when thrifting. This strategy can also appeal to the people who literally ONLY want to thrift, because it involves way more sourcing (which is usually the fun part) and way less marketing (the sometimes not-so-fun part).

Of course, B2B strategies also have disadvantages, which is why a large portion of the thrift army chooses not to go in this direction. A seller to a B2B usually takes a huge opportunity loss when selling their clothing; in other words, if they spent the time processing each item individually, they could reap a much larger profit. If a B2B buyer is incredibly generous, they will pay around 70% of an item's value; I've also experienced stores that will only pay out 7.5% of an item's original retail price. Because of this, a person utilizing this strategy must sell a much larger quantity of product in order to achieve the same profits as a B2C seller. This can become an issue if sourcing locations are limited. These large pay cuts are often enough to deter a seller from going in the B2B direction because if they have the ability to get the full value of an item, they might as well do it.

Personal and outside investments are an inescapable necessity to starting any business, although us thrift kings/queens are often blessed enough to adhere to relatively low investment quotas. 99% of the time, monetary investments in the thrift business are going to be from your own pocket unless you decide to open up a brick-and-mortar, or if you want to open a costly website. The most money I've ever spent in a day of thrifting is probably around $200, and I was able to get almost all of it back within 48 hours. One of the infinitely great things about a thrifting business is that literally ANYONE can likely get the initial investment to start one. I know someone's going to think about that last statement as an entitled and ignorant view on the economic status of individual U.S citizens, but I literally had 5 dollars to my name when I started my Instagram page. I used 4 of those dollars to buy an orange Polo bathing suit, sold that, and reinvested to grow the business which then took off from there. I saw a YouTube video where someone did something similar by starting off with a penny they found on the ground and grew it to over $10,000 within a couple months. A PENNY. The point is, monetary investments are an annoying, necessary, but relatively small part of the thrifting business. You will likely get to the point where you actually want to spend money, because the more money spent translates to more inventory, which in turn brings in more profit. I walk into a thrift store hoping to spend my net worth on clothes, and you should too.

When most people think of the word 'investment', their mind jumps to the assumption that one is talking about the aforementioned monetary investments required to start a business. However, the largest investment that a thrift connoisseur makes is that of something much more invaluable- time. Thrifting is just a single aspect of time consumption when running a business; taking pictures, listing, shipping, advertising, and customer service all take ample amounts of time. Time constraint is one of the largest barriers to entry within the thrifting industry, hands down. Most people simply do not have the time to be running around town without even knowing if they'll find anything. You, the reader, could be struggling with this very problem; after all, we have other responsibilities in life and thrifting tends to be near the bottom of the totem pole (for now). This will likely not be your only job at first, so prior commitments can make this grind seem overwhelming. Because of this, every prospective thrifter must learn to properly organize, structure, and maximize their time consumption to properly suit their business.

Another question that you need to ask yourself is, *"How close are my local thrifts to each other, what is the best route to take when visiting them, and how long will that take me?"* Popping open Google Maps and figuring out the mileage between each thrift can make driving around substantially less time-consuming, and will save gas money as well. Make yourself a mental map to follow in order to maximize efficiency. I have a set route that takes into account distance, importance, and time in order to give me some sense of direction when going out there. It's also important to check the number of thrifts in your area, because unfortunately, the thrift game may just not be possible for you. 19.3% of the world's population lives in rural areas where there will likely not be enough thrift activity for someone to run a business. However, make sure to check the towns within 45-ish minutes of you just to ensure this. A huge portion of my thrifting takes place in a town around 30 minutes from my house because the thrifts there are WAY better. Although this seems like a minor step (which it usually is), it is still of utmost importance to have your route memorized.

Structure. is. imperative. This statement is one of the most important in the book. Structuring your day to conform to the variety of tasks needed to run a business will take a small resale startup to a full-blown thrifting empire. Telling yourself a variant of, '*I'll put three hours aside for thrifting, an hour for listing, an hour for shipping, and another hour for research and growth development*' will make an exponential difference in your business performance. The transformation from random bouts of thrifting to a structured and disciplined battle plan is what turns a hobby to a business. Like, who on earth decides to go into business for themselves and says, *"I'm just gonna wing it every day until I succeed"*? Although that would be really convenient and way cooler than a scheduled day, the hard truth is that winging it is incredibly inefficient. Use a calendar, a notebook, keep it stored in your brain, sharpie the back of your hand, I don't care how you do it. Find a way to be able to go about your day without thinking for a second about what your next move is. It will pay dividends and flips the success switch from 'hard' mode to 'slightly easier but still hard' mode. That's a deceivingly huge difference.

A concept that goes hand in hand with the concept of structure is that of consistency. In order to properly maximize your business efficiency, you must have both. You can't have a well-structured day but only execute it once a week, nor can you go crazy and stupid with no organization for seven days a week. You have to thrift, sell, and deliver items at regular and calculated intervals, without interruption. If Amazon decided to only run their servers twice a week, would they have a trillion-dollar valuation? If Apple was run by a small army of newborn babies with no schedule, would they be able to make revolutionary phones? Those are terrible examples, but the answer to both is probably not! Consistency is definitely one of the most difficult aspects to tackle, for a variety of reasons. Firstly, the temptation to do something else, whether that be hanging out with friends, trying new ventures, etc, is incredibly strong at times. After being in a thrift store for 5 hours, it's human nature to want to go and watch Netflix or something instead. These temptations can likely only be resisted by discipline and the drive to continue striving for success. . Secondly, consistency is difficult because commitment is difficult. I'm sure almost everybody reading this, and definitely the person writing this, have made commitments that they haven't been able to stick to. This is especially true during times of little success, because one's mind starts asking itself, *Is it worth it? Should I quit and move on to something else? Am I even doing this right?* This has personally been one of my biggest trials, but I've learned that it is imperative to gain the confidence and full belief that what you are doing <u>will</u> work, no matter what your brain is screaming at you. I'm sure if you ask basically anybody who has been successful at something, they will tell you that they've considered quitting before. It comes with the game.

A last little detail that may be useful before embarking on your business expenditures is finding the platform in which you plan to sell your items. The right platform will vary widely depending on your chosen niche. One day as I was perusing the art section of a Goodwill out of pure boredom, I found a painting that appeared to be expensive. It had very abstract images of what kind of looked like dandelions but could also be women holding umbrellas but could also be ice cream cones, etc. I had no clue what on earth it was, which is why I figured it was expensive. I looked up the artist, which was luckily pretty easy because the painting had a 'certificate of authenticity' attached to it. After a couple minutes of internet research, I found that the artist's paintings were selling at auction for between $1,000-$6,000. I obviously bought it, thinking that selling it would be as easy as sticking it on eBay for a grand and shipping it out carefully. Unfortunately,

I learned the hard way that eBay is not always the best place to sell art, especially for relatively obscure artists; ones that aren't particularly a 'household name'. I soon found out that selling art involved taking part in a completely different world of auctions, galleries, appraisals, and authentication. Anyway, the moral of this story is that before actually buying things within your niche, I would recommend figuring out which platform is best. Sometimes, it's as easy as setting up an eBay page, but other times the hardest part may be finding a place with buyers.

Hey, look at that! You're a business expert now, ready to jump into your form of transportation and jet over to your modest local thrift palace. BUT WAIT, you're not actually ready yet. The business side of things is important, but it's time to get into the main focus of this text: winning in the thrifts.

Battle Strategies

This section of the book is the reason it was written in the first place. Business knowledge is incredibly important, but 99% of my business-minded friends would waltz into a thrift store and walk out 5 minutes later, empty-handed. Maybe they've researched their niche and end up getting lucky, but let's face it- they don't have the keys to becoming the don, the head honcho, the <u>royalty</u> of that thrift. There are a wide variety of micro-strategies ready to be covered, and it's my job to combine them all into one comprehensive and nearly indestructible battle plan. By the end of this section, you'll be ready to become the person that everyone calls 'lucky' because you find things they don't.

First and foremost, a subject that must be addressed to the utmost importance is time analysis and strategy. This is a fancy term for knowing when, how often, and even <u>if</u> a thrift store should be visited, based off data analysis and personal intuition. Previously mentioned and incredibly necessary time-management skills are unable to be achieved without learning proper time analysis.

In my rookie years, I figured that the time interval in which a thrift store had good items was random. It's natural to assume that a store features expensive items whenever they felt like it, with no rhyme or reason as to why. I would walk in at random times during the day, usually times when I was free or bored, not taking into account at all when the stores were featuring new items. Luckily for you, I realized after thousands of visits just how dumb I was to do this. Most thrifts are actually very methodical with when they release things, especially items of high value. They want the most people possible to see the item, so they generally release things from the depths of the back room during times of heavy foot traffic. This is a characteristic that goes unnoticed with most shoppers, but those who can collect data and analyze it are able to predict when they have the best shot at new items. It's like any statistical frequency analysis; when something happens more often in one time frame than it does another, then there is a better chance of that occurrence happening in the time frame with a better history. For example, since it generally snows frequently during the winter but not often during the summer, the chances of it snowing on a particular day are way higher during the winter months. This same thing can be applied to thrifting; if it usually 'snows' great items at certain times of the day or week, it's obvious that you should visit the thrift stores at those times.

The reason I can't give you a list of times that the thrifts yield the best stuff is that, like snowflakes, no two thrifts are the same. Time analysis is an individual journey in which you must document your own thrift's release tendencies. Documenting and analyzing your data is an endurance race. It will take numerous visits to a thrift to determine its 'money time'. The number one hack I've found so far to speed up the process is consistent communication with the thrift's employees. After all, they work there. They're likely to be in the thrift 4-8 hours a day and one of their main jobs is to feature and 'organize' new items, so a simple question could go a long way. Anything from *"When are you bringing out art next?'* to *"When do you bring out clothing the most often"* can save hours of time and dozens of visits. Whatever you end up asking, make sure to be as nice as possible. As someone who's worked a couple 9 to 5's as well, I know that often times, a little conversation can improve an employee's day a ton. Anyways, picking the best times to visit a thrift can make its 'random' aspect much more predictable.

Initially this is going to seem identical to the topic presented in the last paragraph but is in fact drastically different and essential to time analysis. Every thrift has a different tempo in which they bring out items; some bring products out every twenty minutes while others do every three days. Of course, one always hopes that their primary thrift does the former, but this isn't always the case. There are very few thrifts that are frequent and consistent at the same time, which is why this tip is such a vital one. Determining how often items are brought out in a thrift store is imperative to properly distributing your time. Back to my rookie days. When I was just starting out, my naive self would go to every thrift store, every day without exception. I actually did this up until very recently, because I was so paranoid of missing an item that I would sacrifice hours of my time without acknowledging the opportunity cost. I finally came to the realization that half of the thrifts I visited would only restock every other day, or three days, or week.

I then decided that I had to sacrifice my incessant paranoia in the name of good time management. The lesson here is to create a visitation schedule. Using the same tactics for finding good release times, find out how often new items generally come out. Utilize this data to create a schedule that suits your own thrifting routine. I find it important to point out that sometimes, thrifts require visitation more than once a day. For example, the legendary and elusive 'bins' (we'll get to them later) require almost constant attention. Items fly out of there like planes at an airport, and there can be thousands of individual pieces brought out on an hourly basis. The point is, make sure you're not going to a thrift store too much, but also make sure you're going often enough.

Networking has already been discussed in this book, but on a more 'macro' scale than what the thrifts require. Yeah, networking is important to touch on when discussing business tactics, but it's even MORE important to discuss when we're talking battle strategy. Focusing on the 'micro' of networking (who to talk to and how to talk to them) is a huge key when focusing on the specifics of a thrift store environment. Networking can get you so much further than you already thought, especially when you're in the field.

You may be thinking, *but networking's scary because you have to like, talk to people. I'm not really about that.* Well honestly, you need to be about that. As someone with social anxiety himself, I can relate to you on how frightening approaching a random person can be. I still struggle with it myself sometimes. What I can tell you is, a majority of the time, simply asking a question will go to your benefit. Maybe they'll say no, but your social skills will improve every time, and hopefully your confidence will as well. Every time you get cold feet before approaching a person, think, *that person could be the key to success for me. Simply talking to them could open doors to me that I couldn't even fathom before.* There have been many times where a conversation has gone significantly further than I expected and resulted in a huge benefit for me. Make the jump, it's one of many that are required to achieve business success.

A first subcategory of networking is that between you and your local thrift employees. The people working in a thrift are often super nice and want to help their customers in any way possible. I feel like people often see store employees as sort of an emotionless non-human whose only job is to serve them, and they treat them according to this false generalization. Because of this, being a kind, personable, and engaging customer results in a significant advantage over the usual entitled loser. Help from employees may be the single biggest advantage an individual can have when thrifting; they can give you access to lands unknown by the everyday shopper. When thinking about the setup of a thrift store, it becomes obvious to what advantages a thrift store employee can give you. For example, they can override your time analysis by simply bringing out items when you ask them to. They're often the only people with the ability to access the fabled 'back room', where a literal treasure trove is stored for the picking.

As I was talking about the back room just there, I realized that I really need to put an emphasis on the importance of this space. The back room is any thrifter's dream; there's literally (at least) double a store's inventory, not yet searched through, and not yet priced. However, accessing the backroom is like trying to find a romantic partner in a room full of supermodels- there's still a chance, but it's gonna take a ton of social skills and failure before you get there. From my experience, thrift stores that aren't part of a Goodwill-like chain are your best bet when trying to access this thrifter's mecca. The managers and employees in chain thrifts are trained to not grant customers this opportunity, so going to an independently-run thrift gives you a better chance.

Ok, back to the employee networking thing. Another advantage in befriending someone working inside the thrift is help in locating things. An employee will be more likely to help you find something within the store if you're friends with them already. For people with social anxiety, it's also WAY easier to ask them for things during a bout of small talk; having a conversation about the weather and then being like "oh yeah by the way do you have any military tanks" is easier than just walking up to them and saying it upfront.

Employees are also super good with finding things in a particular niche, especially after they see your buying patterns. I always figured employees didn't notice a pattern in what I was buying, until a store manager asked me if I wanted more vintage clothes and proceeded to take me to a treasure trove in the back room. If you get to know an employee, they'll get to know you. It's a symbiotic relationship; you get free money while the employee gets some entertainment in their day, and you both get a friendship. It makes thrifting a heck of a lot easier and turns your trips into a minor social event as well. It's honestly really nice being able to walk into any establishment and get special treatment, so why not capitalize on it as well?

Woohoo, so you've gotten to know the employees. Seriously though, this is a huge step in the networking process within a thrift. However, it only accounts for half of the socializing you need to take part in. The other half, of course, is with the only other people in there- the customers.

Getting to properly know your fellow customers within a thrift, especially the frequent ones, is incredibly helpful when trying to source items for your particular niche. A thrift is like an ecosystem in itself; everybody is in there looking for something, and if you know what everyone else is looking for, you can use this to your advantage. I can't even count the amount of times that one of my fellow thrifters has walked up to me with an item that they knew I wanted in my cart. A system of trade is frequent within a high-traffic store because trading inside the store requires no monetary investment. For example, I know a woman in one of my regular stores that looks fervently for purses. That's literally all she looks for. However, she's started to look for vintage clothing as well because she knows that although I've got an eye for purses, but they're not really my niche. If I ever find a decent purse, I know to go to her because she may have something that tickles my fancy. This nifty little business trick can basically give you rule over the entire store, and you don't have to worry as much about people taking items that you want.

Just like most networking interactions, you can learn a TON from talking to other people within a thrift store. I remember thinking I was literally the Albert Einstein of vintage clothes at one point. I was convinced that nobody could teach me anything that I didn't know about my niche (close-minded, I know). Around 6 months ago, I met a guy in the Goodwill bins that, like me, bought and sold vintage clothes for a living. He spent up to 8 hours a day at the bins, and I began to spend a ton of time in there as well. One day, a bin of shoes came out and I observed him while he picked up every pair of Converses in sight and kept looking in the inside of them. To my knowledge, Converses were worth close to nothing in used condition, so I asked him why he even bothered. He explained to me that Converses that said 'Made in the USA' on the inside were sometimes worth hundreds of dollars, and that he once paid a couple months of rent from a bin of them. I was floored. I had absolutely no clue this was a thing, and I've been looking at the insides of Converse ever since. As time went on, he kept revealing similar tricks to me. Whether it was a capital 'E' on a Levi's jeans tab or that some John Deere hats were worth $100, he would drop knowledge to me on a daily basis. His advice alone has yielded me hundreds of dollars in the past couple of months, and all of this money came from simply talking to him. From my experience, people in general like to share their secrets from thrifting because it shows their extensive knowledge on their niche. It gives them a sense of accomplishment to reveal their achievement of finding out something that most people don't know. A single person can often give you more information on your niche than a book can (other than this one, of course).

Customer interaction is also great because it makes the job a bit less lonely. Having a conversation while waiting for new items to come out can make the time fly by much quicker. Everybody has their own story and listening to the varying tales that people have can be super interesting. I honestly feel like I've become a more culturally aware person by thrifting; the sheer diversity of the people that I talk to everyday really gives me a worldly perspective of life. I've met the rich, the poor, and every socioeconomic class in between. I've met veterans, construction workers, business owners, and first generation immigrants. Knowing the struggles and accomplishments of people dissimilar to you is one of the most valuable things a thrift can offer. Money is always worth a set value; experiences and information are priceless.

Positioning, positioning, positioning. It's the king of all battle strategies. In basketball, positioning yourself in between the opponent and the basket is the best defensive strategy. In 19th-century France, Napoleon used a revolutionary form of troop positioning to help take over a quarter of the world. Putting yourself in the right situation is generally helpful for almost everything in life, and like almost every life concept I've brought up so far in this book, thrifting is not an exception to the rule. Placing yourself in an area where the chances of finding something are higher is a major key. If we're carrying the war metaphor a bit further here, the store layout is the battlefield, and anybody else in the store is the opponent. Yes, I know they're probably really nice people and I still encourage you to talk to them, but that doesn't take away from the fact that they could lose you money. Positioning can help you battle these fellow shoppers effectively and take what's rightfully yours. Take a dominant stance in the store by letting everybody know you mean business. I'll give an example.

In the Goodwill bins, the epitome of raw human nature being confined to a given space, there are generally people that assert themselves as dominant by simply positioning themselves properly. In my local example, I have the 'shoe lady'. She's at least six foot two, heavyset, and is a generally terrifying person. Her main objective is shoes (hence the very fitting name), and she tends to mill around the other bins until new shoes are brought out. Once the shoe bins are brought out, she sprints with cheetah-like speed to the best spot possible and makes sure that <u>nobody</u> comes even close to taking the valuable shoes. She takes the best shoes in the bin, sells them to third-world countries, and makes a full living off it. Although people don't really like her, it's only because when she shows up, they know that there is no way their submissive nature will work anymore. If they want shoes, they're gonna have to square up. The moral of this story is, be the shoe lady. You may not be an absolute unit of a person like her, but the mindset can get you pretty far anyway.

When learning to learning to situate yourself as properly as you can in a thrift, there are a few rules to abide by. The first one of these imperative rules is to know <u>exactly</u> where you're going within the first couple seconds of you walking into the store. Although they often seem useless, those opening seconds can mean the difference between finding a gem and coming out as a failure. You need to enter the doors of that establishment with purpose. Having a clear idea on where you want to go when you get into the store increases your chances in finding free money and saves priceless minutes where you would otherwise be wandering aimlessly. The best way to figure this out is really to just like, look. Thrifts have their own spaces for everything; books, records, clothes, weapons of mass destruction, whatever. The best place to rush to when walking into a thrift store is the place where your niche resides. If you're looking for clothes, go to the new clothes racks. If you're looking for records, go to the boxes of records. You want to create a hierarchy of importance when meandering a thrift; figure out which places are best to find items and visit them in order of potential. Although there are often places where there is almost zero chance of finding something that's up your alley, I would still recommend going through the entire store. I've found gems in the weirdest of spots, and they're usually there because someone hid them in the area least likely to be sifted through.

Speaking of hiding things, make sure to figure out the popular hiding spots inside a thrift store as well. Almost every busy thrift has them, and if you haven't found the one in yours yet, there are probably valuable items just feet from you without you noticing. In the thrift closest to my house, there was a hiding spot in the corner of the store, where people would put stuff behind the men's suits. Whoever came up with the spot was a genius; you could not see <u>anything</u> behind the suits, the suits were already an unpopular niche in the store, and they were stored in a place with very low foot traffic. I actually discovered it myself when trying to hide an item that I was going to later come back for. There was literally a cart's worth of new-in-box electronics back there. Free money. I started checking there every time I went to that store, and I found things back there at least half of the times I checked. These hiding spots can be honey holes, so finding them can be an extra little perk for each thrift visit.

As I said before, the items in the back room are potentially untapped gold. Your best chance, by far, at finding anything good is to acquire an item before most people even have the chance to see it. This concept is why you need to <u>immediately</u> rush over when there are new items brought out by employees. Be almost obnoxious about it. If there's a pair of shoes in a cart being brought out and there's even a slight chance you might want them, make sure to hover over them like a vulture. Even ask the employee for them. Verbally call dibs if there are other people eyeing them. Being politically correct does not have a place when new items are at stake. People might be slightly annoyed by it, but it's usually out of jealousy because they don't have the courage to take initiative and get what they want. A personal favorite of mine is to just put my body in front of the item and basically do a defensive box-out until the employee has officially put it out. It doesn't even give the shopper a chance to see what I'm going after; they're left up to guessing what amazing item I've found this time. It's a jungle out there, so use body language to assert dominance and make them dread having you in there. I would recommend still being a nice person verbally, though. As I previously mentioned in the networking section, making friends can be very useful, and being verbally obnoxious will likely throw any friendship into jeopardy.

You thought I couldn't bring up the back room again? Well, you're wrong. Because it's important. If you plan on being in a thrift store for a relatively extended period of time, positioning yourself near the doors of the back room is a solid choice. By doing this, you're able to do a number of beneficial things. Firstly, you can take a peek back there and see what sort of items are coming out; this can be a good indicator of whether you should stay in the store and wait for new things or not. If your niche is books and there are nothing but live eels coming out in the near future, there's probably no reason for you to be there any longer. Or for anybody to be there, in that case. Secondly, you get to be the first person to see newly-featured items. You can use your newly-taught boxing out technique in a very effective fashion if you're the first person to see things. Also, the employee could be nice and toss the item at you when they see you drooling at it. There's usually chairs in thrifts, so throwing down a chair near the ominous doors of the back room and sitting around there isn't an awful idea.

While I was creating a structure for the thrifting strategies section of this book, I was left with a few key points that didn't necessarily fall under any specific subcategory. There was absolutely no way I could leave these out, because they represent some intangible, less straightforward strategies that I have found to be incredibly effective in my thrift endeavors. After a couple minutes of putting my brain into overdrive trying to find a loose connection between all of my points, I decided to just throw them in a 'miscellaneous tips' category. So yeah, here's that.

A major key to succeeding in a thrift setting is what I call "keeping your eyes on your own paper". This is usually used by teachers for when you and your friend are copying each other's Spanish test because you forgot all of those stupid conjugations. However, the 'paper' I'm referring to in this instance is money. Focus on yourself when you're thrifting, at least to a degree. In other words, don't get obsessed with what other people are finding; do your own thing. I can't even count the amount of times that someone has grabbed a valuable item from right under my nosc because I was too busy looking over at somebody else while trying to piece together what they had found. I remember one time, I was sifting through a bin of clothes half-heartedly while looking at a guy probe through the bin across from me. It seemed like he was finding a good bit of clothes, so I moved over to his bin instead. He simultaneously shifted over to my bin, switching with me. He then pulled out five insanely cool pieces of clothing from the bin I was literally just standing in front of. The bin that I was now positioned over was empty. If I'd kept my eyes on my own paper, I wouldn't have missed out on it. This is really a concept that can be applied to most things in life, because jealousy often results in self-destruction. You thought this book only spit thrift facts? Nope, you're getting whole life lessons out here. Crazy value.

The biggest component to thrifting is, of course, the thrifts themselves. They house the very treasure you search for; they're absolutely essential to your success. To get to the point I'm about to make, let me give you an analogical situation. You're in charge of a diamond mining company in which you look for the next 'honey hole' of diamonds in order to turn a profit. One day, you find the ultimate digging site. There are diamonds galore, and nobody within the mining industry seems to be aware of it. You reap a ton of initial success, and you're almost positive that this mine can be a source of long-term economic prosperity to you. One day, you pull up to a bar in your new diamond-encrusted Lamborghini to hang out with some friends. Your one friend goes, "I just have to ask. Where are you getting all of this money? Where are you mining these days to reap such a crazy profit?" My question to you is, would you tell him about where your honey hole is? If your answer to this question is no (which I hope it is for the purpose of this analogy), then you've made the right financial decision. No matter how strong the amount of peer pressure is, you should try to keep those beneficial secrets to be just that, a secret. Of course, the same can be applied to thrifting. Some thrifts are just better than others. That's just how it is. One of the factors that determines the quality of a thrift store is the amount of traffic it brings every day. The less traffic, the less competition. This is why it's absolutely essential that you keep your good spots a secret. I've made the mistake of doing this one too many times; my town is now teeming with dozens of daily thrift visitors looking for the same thing as me. They know which stores to go to, where to look in the stores, what times to go to the store, and how long to stay in there. This is all because I made the mistake of not keeping my mouth shut. The lesson here is, don't let people leech off of your hard work. Keep your treasure troves secret instead of sacrificing future income just for the sake of bragging.

Yesterday (at least, for me; you're probably reading this way later), I was going through a Goodwill when I found a record player. I've always had an interest in record players, and this one in particular had finally matched the aesthetic that I wanted my room to have. It was (supposedly) brand new in the box, had all of the proper packaging, and had absolutely zero cosmetic blemishes or detriments of any kind. I figured, hey, this is a new record player. Someone must have bought it or received it as a gift and decided that they didn't want it anymore. I figured that because of this, I didn't have to test it out. Goodwills usually have a couple of outlets in the store to allow the testing of electronics and appliances, but I felt I was too busy to bother. I took the record player home, absolutely elated to test it out with the random free-form jazz record that I bought with it. Yeah, you guessed it. It was broken. Although it was kind of the donator's fault because they donated a BROKEN record player, I took the blame. After all, I had broken something as well- one of my essential rules of buying secondhand goods. Always check for flaws. If it's clothes, look for stains, rips, or undesirable features. If it's electronics, check to see if every aspect of it is in working condition. If it's a puzzle, lego set, or something similar, make sure every part comes with it. If you buy an item that doesn't have the features that people are looking for, they obviously won't buy it, resulting in an unnecessary loss for you. Lost money is one of the only types of money that nobody wants.

This one isn't really a cautionary guideline or anything, more like a cool Easter egg of thrifting that could potentially skyrocket your profits. I've mentioned the 'bins' a couple times so far in this guide, but really only referred to them as a mystical oasis of free money. Which it is. I promise. The 'bins' are formally known as the Goodwill Clearance Center. Think of the process like this. Goodwill receives WAY more donations than you see in the stores. Like, the stores only account for around a quarter of what they bring in, if that. Goodwill randomly assign piles of donations to certain areas. The Goodwill retail centers (the normal stores) sort through, clean up, and properly present the donations so that they look less 'used'. The Goodwill Clearance is different. They categorize the donations, but do not sort through, clean up, or present the donations in a proper fashion. Instead, they throw them into large bins and roll them out as a glorious pile of mystery. Already amazing, right? Well, we're just getting started. There are a countless number of advantages to this particular kind of thrift. Firstly, there's the aforementioned massive bins of clothes instead of pre-sorted racks of a limited number. Secondly, the bins come out in groups of four, eight, twelve, or sixteen. Each bin has at least 30-50 items in it, and way more if we're talking books. This means that there's a potential for thousands of items in a release. The extreme excess of inventory being let out of the back room than most people can even handle. Also, they let out those bins constantly. I'm talking every 15 minutes, if you come at the right time. They're letting out a full store's inventory every couple of hours, and it's all new.

You may be thinking, *I can't afford all of that inventory! Thrifts charge pretty high prices per item, even if you're buying in bulk.* Nope. The Goodwill Clearance charges your haul by the pound. Screw all of that piece-by-piece crap. They toss your gold mine onto a scale and charge you $1.19 a pound. There have been times where I've walked out of the store and felt like I just robbed it. It really doesn't seem fair if I'm being honest. Due to the abysmally low inventory costs, people pile up their carts like there's no tomorrow.

Obviously, every utopia still has its faults. First of all, the Clearance is a jungle. Every time a new set of bins is brought out, people flock it like a pack of hungry wolves. I've seen multiple fights over items and have almost been a part of one myself. It was over a pair of Gucci shoes and I saw them first, so I don't really regret it. Anyway, the populous in there is usually a competitive bunch; the people residing in my local bins are there every day, no matter the circumstances. I've never been there during a hurricane, but if Goodwill decided to stay open during a category five for some reason, I can almost guarantee you that the clearance gang would be sifting through bins per the usual. This means that your thrifting prowess has to be in overdrive because there are individuals there with just as much intention and skill as you. Additionally, the bins are few and far-between. There's a good chance that you aren't within a hundred miles of them, and if there happens to be one, it likely won't be in an ideal part of town. Goodwill tries to upkeep a certain reputation as a thrift chain, and the bins are usually just a way to profit off of excess inventory before sending the rest to rag houses. If you happen to be blessed with a bins near you, take advantage of them. Do it in the name of your fellow thrifters in rural Kansas with a single thrift store hidden in a cornfield 30 miles away. They would kill for one of those in their town, and if they did have one, they'd probably have to kill someone anyway so they can get that cool sweater they saw in a bin.

As a summation of the copious amounts of knowledge I have just bestowed upon you, correctly navigating a thrift is vastly more complex than what generally meets the eye. This book isn't trying to make you reinvent the wheel, just improve it. Yes, you can walk into a thrift store with no intention or direction and still find valuable things. That's not what I am trying to disprove. You can, though, find way more valuable items when conducting an effective strategy such as this one when in a thrift setting. Strategy is behind almost every great success in this world; a lot of people think thrift stores are an exception to this rule. These same people view a thrift as a 'lottery' opportunity instead of a consistent source of income, and that's where they're getting it wrong. You can do both. By employing these strategies, you can formulate a base income while also reaping the benefits of the occasional lucky find. The section you just completed is the meat of this book and is the reason I decided to write it in the first place. However, applying this knowledge to a business environment is still imperative. I've already given you some general base knowledge on how to prepare for starting the next thrift Amazon, but the next step to success is actually applying it.

Initiating Money Moves

The previous business section was meant to outline the steps needed to form a foundation for your soon-to-be empire, but the real work is in building, scaling, and automating the business to fit your particular goals. Let's be honest, almost anyone can <u>start</u> a business. What separates a lemonade stand from Amazon is, among other things, persistence and growth. Warren Buffett once said "the stock market is a device for transferring money from the patient to the impatient". The same can be said for business. Patience is an absolute necessity in any business venture. Tesla didn't make its first car until ten years after the company's fabrication. Amazon started by selling books. Every major corporation started with a vision in mind; founders had the patience to execute that vision effectively, which is why these companies are so successful today. This next section outlines some key steps to taking a newly-minted thrift business from zero to hero, all while following the vision that you, Mr./Ms. Reader, had in mind from the beginning.

Regardless of the business model you choose, one of the most important things to figure out after sourcing items is what's called a listing technique. This is a strategy for when you're finally ready to throw your items on to your selling platform of choice. You B2B folks may be a bit confused as to why you need to know this, but you have to remember that 99% of the time, not everything you're trying to sell to other businesses is going to sell. You have the option to either take a full loss on the item or to leak a bit into the consumer realm and get selling. Anyway, a listing technique is how you go about posting items onto whatever selling platform(s) you ultimately choose. You have to look at listing from a ton of different angles; the title, the description, the photos, the price, the list goes on. Your chances of selling an item rise exponentially when you post what the customer wants to see. The actual item listing is a form of marketing in itself, and mastering the art of listing can take a business to the next level.

One aspect of listing, and one that can be the most important depending on the niche, is taking pictures of the item. In any market, buyers want to know what they're purchasing. A general rule to follow is the more pictures, the better. The three keys to taking good pictures of your item are clarity, artistry, and detail. Clarity is relatively simple; the pictures have to be clear enough for the buyer to see. Make sure to use the best camera you have access to in order to capture the sharpest image of your product. Artistry involves the overall aesthetics of the picture. You want to get the best angles possible of the item; this doesn't mean you should hide any flaws but try to make the item look as appealing as possible. It's like taking a picture of yourself. If you take a selfie from a terrible angle with terrible lighting, you're probably not gonna look as good as your potential allows you. Just the truth. However, if you take that selfie with professional grade lighting at an appealing angle, you're going to the cover of Vogue. Also, try to stage the item in an interesting setting to make the listing look a bit more ~artsy~. For example, I know of a lot of people in my vintage clothing niche that buy fake grass/turf and take pictures of the clothing laid out on the grass. This makes the article of clothing pop and gives the post a cool, nature-like aesthetic. The third, and arguably the most critical aspect of capturing your item, is making sure to include every vital detail. This is a very subjective thing to tackle; every item has its own unique features, and it's up to you to figure out what parts of the item to highlight. Put yourself in the position of the buyer and ask yourself, *what parts of this product would I find helpful to be included in the listing?* This usually helps me to look at the item from a consumer's perspective. A crucial, more objective rule to taking pictures of an item is to always include pictures of any flaws. Consumers always want to see what a flaw looks like. Sometimes they are willing to still purchase the item even with flaws, but they will always want to see what they're getting themselves into. Basically, make sure to put a ton of attention into pictures. Don't lazily throw your item on to a couch and snap 3 pictures. Pictures are worth a thousand words, and can also be worth thousands of dollars if you do it right.

The title of a listing is also crucially important. It can catch a consumer's eye and inform them of what they're about to click on; think of it as a first impression when meeting someone. That's a pretty obvious reason as to why a title can be important, but there are other, less apparent ways that titles affect the sale of your item. One of these is through algorithms. The algorithms in most websites use keywords to categorize your item and properly put it in a list for the user, in an order where the most relevant results are at the top. The best way for your item to appear at the top of web searches is by the use of 'descriptors': terms of importance that both effectively and accurately describe your item. For example, say I'm trying to sell a pair of Jordan 4's. I'm not going to use 'Jordan 4' as my title; it won't be anywhere near the top of any search page. I'm going to use the brand, shoe, size, gender, model, and maybe even the serial number. My 'Jordan 4' will now instead be 'Nike Air Jordan 4 White Cement Men's Size 11.5 840606-192'. The goal is to effectively target the people looking for this exact shoe. This sounds kind of counterintuitive because some would think, *I need to use a broad title because more people are going to search 'Jordan 4' than they are 'Nike Jordan 4 White Cement blah blah blah'.* Although this may be true, marketing is about making the product easy to find for the people looking <u>for that exact product</u>, not just a product in its genre. Using an effective title gives the buyer a good first impression to the product, and we all know how important a first impression can be.

The 'description' section of a listing is the equivalent of a witness explaining in court what they saw during a crime- you should include every notable detail you can possibly remember. Buyers love when a seller includes extensive details about their product because it increases their buyer's security. Purchasing things on the internet is still scary to some, so make sure they feel informed and safe about what they're buying. This includes the condition, the physical details, whether the item 'works' or not, the features that the item comes with, and any flaws whatsoever. Basically, just rant about your product until your brain can't come up with anything else to say about it. Another key to writing a description is to always be completely truthful and accurate about everything involving the product. Trust me, customers will <u>not</u> hesitate to return their item, give you a bad review, or try to get your page taken down. Any of these outcomes is a huge hassle, so being honest and thorough with your descriptions is quite frankly the easiest path to take.

The next aspect of a listing is the detail that almost every customer is going to care about- price. Pricing an item to satisfy both you and the customer can be tricky. Sellers and buyers alike can be stubborn when participating in a transaction, so finding a price that makes everybody happy is the ideal situation. From what I've experienced, the best way to price an item is by using one (or two) of two things- what the item has sold for in the past, and the prices of current listings for the same item. Picking which price to base your listing off of generally revolves around how much patience you have when selling it. If you want to get rid of an item very quickly, try to find what price the item has been consistently selling for, and price it either at that price, or slightly under it. If you have time to wait, price it for what other sellers are selling it for right now. However, there is a third option- using a vague average of the previous sell prices <u>and</u> the current listing prices. This is personally my favorite option because I've found that I can sell items relatively quickly while still getting a solid return on my investment. I find a happy medium between what the item is selling for and what the 'market price' is. For example, if I see that a pair of shoes has previously sold for $50 but there are eBay listings that have it at $100, I'll put it up for between $60 and $80. This helps get rid of the item faster while still yielding a profit that satisfies me. Pricing as a whole comes down to an analysis of your own patience and willingness to negotiate.

So, I'm going to assume that, after taking in this plethora of knowledge from the chapter so far, you are now able to competently make a sale. I hope you've found it to be even easier than you expected. Anyway, you're definitely not done after you receive the sale notification on your phone. The money that's sitting in your bank from the sale is known as 'unearned revenue'; that is, it technically isn't yours until you have completed the transaction. In order for the money to be your new and fully-reaped reward for all of that hard work, you need to complete the transaction. As long as nothing else goes awry, this just means you need to ship that baby out and wait for your mail service of choice to work its magic. However, there are some specifics in shipping that are important to mention to ensure that everything goes to plan.

Shipping as a concept (and usually as an action, too) is a pretty easy job. You really just need to throw your item into a parcel and send it out. However, it is a critical step in the reselling process and also the step in which you likely have the most to lose. Improper and inefficient shipping techniques can result in unexpected losses that really never needed to happen. In order to prevent this, there are a few steps that you can follow to make sure that your parcel could survive even if a nuclear bomb happened to strike the UPS truck or something.

Firstly, always keep your tracking numbers. Tracking numbers are major key to making sure you get the money you deserve quickly and easily. I personally shove them all into that weird pocket that most cars have in the back of the driver and passenger seat, but a box or a folder would likely be more effective. Tracking numbers are the number one way to deter eBay scammers. Without one, a buyer can easily appeal their purchase and you'll never see your money or item again. The ONE time I forgot to add a tracking number to a purchase, the buyer claimed that I never shipped the item out. Because of this, I had to refund him $150 and I never saw the shoes again. $150 could buy me 37.5 Wendy's 4 for 4 meals, which means I could have eaten Wendy's for 12.5 days straight if I didn't make that crucial mistake. Hate to see it. Although my arteries probably didn't.

Secondly, make sure to use the proper packaging. That sounds pretty obvious, but sometimes finding the correct box for an item is difficult and you're gonna want to cut corners. I have had far too many boxes break open and almost cost me a sale simply because the item didn't properly fit in a box. If the box is too small, the item can fly around and either break the item or the box. If it's too big, same thing except for the flying around part. I'd recommend finding a sturdy box, too. If you can't put a pretty heavy item on top of the box without it breaking, it's probably not going to survive the violent process of being shipped across the country.

Finally, tape intelligently and tape a <u>lot</u>. When I have an expensive item to ship out, I cover that box with more tape than it would take to fully assemble an aircraft. I make sure that item would survive if it was fired from a cannon into your house instead of delivered by truck. I wrap that box with more tape than the amount of cloth it took for the Egyptians to wrap their mummies. In actuality though, it's important to tape a box sturdily and in the right way. Using the 'H method', where you tape each of the creases to form an 'H' shape on both the top and bottom of the box is considered to be the most effective and efficient way to do it. You've made it too far to mess up now, gotta make sure to stay on your toes and keep that money up.

So yeah, those last couple of paragraphs were a detailed way to say 'make sure to secure your items properly', but I felt that it was important to be more specific because those losses can cause a huge hit to your profits. It was worth your time, trust me.

When my business started to pick up, I realized that I had no idea how much money I was actually making. My bank account was constantly fluctuating due to personal purchases and business sales, so it was nearly impossible to keep track of it in my head. Knowing what numbers I was putting up was important to me because, like almost any profession, knowing what you're earning and what you can do to make more is a key to growth. I made a spreadsheet and began writing down everything I bought, how much it cost me, and how much I sold it for. Let me tell you, it was like giving a person with a sight deficiency glasses for the first time. I was finally able to see clearly what aspects of my business were working, what needed to be improved, and how my business was performing overall at any given time. Keeping track of your cash flow gives you a huge advantage when looking to improve your business. It's easy to see what items bring in the most profit and which ones you should start avoiding. I took a class that outlined some of the basics to using spreadsheet programs (Excel, Google Sheets, etc.) and realized that it's actually quite simple to automate your record-keeping. I would recommend doing some research on how to use spreadsheet equations to help with calculating key numbers such as profit margins, cost per item, and average selling price. There are a million ways to organize your records, but it should really be in a way that makes the most sense to you. It's also nice to see your overall numbers go up, and it's really easy to set goals for yourself when the information is right in front of you. For example, if your average profit margin is at 45 percent and you want to make it 50, you can receive instant feedback on whether a business decision would get you closer to that goal or not. Keeping records is a huge money move that doesn't require much additional work to achieve.

In the reselling world, a seller's entire business depends on thcir customer reviews. Having a good rating on your selling platform can make you skyrocket to the top or cut your customer base in half. The entirety of your reputation relies on how you treat your customers. If your customer orders a TV from you and you decide to send them a can of tuna instead, there's a good chance that person is not going to buy from you again unless they're a cat. If you send them the TV quickly and efficiently, that customer will likely notice how well you did and may consider purchasing from you again. Customer service as a whole can be summed up by one sentence- always put the customer first. The customer is how you're making your living, so attending to their needs in a methodical and productive manner will help them turn into a repeat customer. Additionally, the customer's reviews of your services could assist in persuading other prospective buyers into purchasing your product. Customers will inevitably have a few problems with your services every once in a while, but the way you handle their responses will determine your prowess as a seller. If Mr. Customer

Man is upset because his product didn't arrive as described, make sure to stay in constant communication with them and make sure of two things. Firstly, determine whether it was your fault. People can scam you all the time, so you want to make sure that although you're treating the customer well, you're not treating them <u>too</u> well. Secondly, if it is your fault, make sure you attend to their needs in a way that makes it super easy for the buyer. Nobody wins when you ignore a customer's complaint; people will often hold you accountable if you refuse to listen to them. Make sure to satisfy your clientele to the best of your ability. A happy customer makes a happy seller.

Participating in your niche's community is another essential part of building your business. Every niche has a community; I've realized that no matter how random or specific your niche may be, there's probably a Reddit forum or something revolving around it. Members of the community are often experts on certain sub-categories in your niche as well. For example, I know a guy that knows absolutely everything about vintage Nike tees. When I have a question about a Nike item, he's gonna know the answer. If he doesn't, the answer must be locked up in a Nike vault or something because this guy's a guru. The point is, figuring out the answers to problems, especially ones revolving around your niche, is way easier when you're an active member of the community. Answering other people's questions, showing off your finds, or just helping people in any way possible will allow you to make a plethora of connections. Help people, they'll help you back.

At this point, you've been educated in just about everything you need to get you through the early days of your business, but there's one imperative attribute that has yet to be acknowledged: growth. Scaling your business is the part where you turn your little household business into a full operation. It's a process that takes patience, work, and a lot of business knowledge to perform. It's what turned McDonalds from a small drive-through in San Bernardino into the largest restaurant chain in the world. It's what took Steve Jobs and Steve Wozniak out of their garage and into the history books. Need more examples? Look at literally any major company. They all required scaling to get to the level in which they are currently residing. However, thrifting is a business that can be somewhat tricky to scale because of the laborious and limited sourcing involved. Most companies do not have to tackle this specific obstacle because they have a virtually unlimited source of their product. For instance, if Yeti Coolers begins to get more sales than before, they can simply make more Yeti Coolers. If your thrifting business takes off, finding more items can sell is exponentially more difficult. Luckily, there's still a way to grow.

I'm going to talk about the most obvious way to scale first so you can rest your mind knowing that I've mentioned it- you can hire people to thrift for you. You're only one person, which means you can only be in one place at a time. If you have multiple thrifts in your area, it's just about impossible to get every good item from every thrift. But let's say you have a bunch of thrifts locally. If you hire a person to sit in every thrift waiting for new items to come out, you have almost total control on everything coming out of those back room doors. You may be thinking, *but why would people work for me if they could just do it themselves and run their own business*? I thought the same thing myself; it's the next logical thought. However, some people simply don't want to deal with the business side of things. They'd rather sit in the thrifts all day and search; they're thrifting purists who simply enjoy the thrill of the hunt. They're willing to sacrifice a couple bucks in order to avoid the headaches of running a business. The same thing can be said for listing. Some people don't want to get their hands dirty and would rather sit at a computer and make listings all day instead of running around. Both types of people can be extremely beneficial to you, and there are more of them than you would think. Throwing up a basic internet ad can turn up some pretty good employees, especially if you take some time to teach them the thrifting techniques that you've learned.

Of course, the obvious downside to hiring employees is that they cost money. Some businesses are simply not at the level where they can profitably hire employees; some are faster than others to reach this point. Record keeping can help determine whether you can afford it. To figure out if it's the right financial decision for your business, you have to estimate how much revenue a single employee could generate and then use that prediction to see what pay rate you could afford. The two most popular ways to pay employees are usually by the piece and by the hour. I prefer by the piece; it allows you to pay the employee only when they've performed well and it gives them more incentive to work hard. Of course, you have to make sure that your employee knows the niche well or at least shows expertise in internet research. Regardless, hiring employees could help you in taking a massive step in the right direction if you're confident that your company is in the right position to do so.

Expanding into other markets outside of your niche can be another lucrative step toward scaling. I didn't want to bring this next step up until now out of fear that you would ignore my emphasis on researching a niche, so hopefully you'll still do that because it IS important. I know that earlier, I said that I strongly believe that the niche system is superior to trying to be a 'jack of all trades'. This is still true. However, if you've already spent a significant amount of time within a niche, expanding and researching additional niches can widen your horizons. For example, I spent 2 years working almost exclusively in vintage and designer clothing. I barely even looked at anything else. Once I felt confident that I had fully mastered it, I began moving into electronic appliances as well. Because I ran an eBay store that didn't really have a certain niche tied to it, I was able to increase profits. It proved to be a solid move and unlocked a completely new section of the thrifts for me to explore.

Sometimes, expanding into the realm of infinite niches can be counterintuitive. There are only certain situations in which it can work out. In other instances, it can actually reduce your brand, customer base, and profitability. For example, let's say you run an Instagram page that focuses on selling shoes. You've amassed a large following of people that are interested in buying shoes. One day, you decide that you want to start selling exotic lizards as well. More likely than not, you are going to lose a huge portion of your following because the people following you are looking for shoes, not a multicolored gecko. Which doesn't make much sense because geckos are really cool, but that's just not how the world works. Anyway, that example is a situation in which you should not spread to other niches unless you want to open up an entirely separate store. Widening your horizons can be good for certain businesses, but you don't see Microsoft selling coffee for a reason. Before making a decision to add product categories, make sure your business is right for it. Like most business decisions, it can result in huge losses if you don't do it the right way.

As I was browsing through Instagram a couple of days ago, I found this guy who had a self-proclaimed obsession with putting his face on billboards. He would throw his face on one billboard with a link to his music, another with his Instagram, and of course, one with him asking a girl to prom. How else would you do it? At first this may sound like a really random waste of money, but I saw it as absolute genius. The guy had garnered almost 20,000 Instagram followers when I checked, all because he threw his face on some billboards. He had news teams interviewing him, celebrities shouting him out, and people from across the country showing him love. He advertised himself in a unique way, and it paid off. In business, advertising can have just as much of an effect as it did for the billboard guy. It can scale a company from relative obscurity into a household name. Clothing companies have celebrities wear their clothes, electronics companies showcase a video of their product, and Instagram users put themselves on billboards. Advertising is the obvious key to making a business more popular and increasing revenue.

There are a million ways to do it, but the most important part is making it creative and eye-catching. Nobody wants to look at a boring ad. I doubt you can remember a single boring ad that you've ever watched. However, if you can entertain the viewer while simultaneously informing them of your business, you've succeeded. That's the whole point of doing it. I don't want to go too deep into the specifics of advertising because 1. It could be a book in itself and 2. You should strategize in a way that's best for you, but I wanted to at least address it as a crucial way to scale a business. The point is, let people know about your business in the most cost-conscious way possible. An effective ad campaign could be one of the best things you ever did for your business.

In my opinion, money moves have certainly been initiated. I really just wanted to form a broad base for the business you're building because, after all, it's your business. You're the one that's building it, and you're the one that's going to ultimately make the decisions. All I'm doing is suggesting and guiding. There's that old saying that comes to mind for me, "Give a man a fish, feed him for a day. Teach a man to fish, feed him for a lifetime". This really resonates with the point I'm trying to get across. I didn't want to order you around and tell you exactly what moves you should make, that doesn't teach you anything. The only thing it teaches you is to follow orders. I wanted to give you some recommendations and let you build your empire on your own. Trust me, it's much more rewarding and

you'll learn much more than a book
could ever teach you.

Epilogue

The thrifts can be a magical place. If you've learned anything from this book, I hope it's that. It's created a career for thousands of people around the globe and strikes adventure in the hearts of those looking for excitement in their day. My intention of this book was to accomplish a few things.

Firstly, I wanted to either make you aware of a thrift's advantages, or amplify them if they're already there. In my opinion, it's one of the few places where almost anyone can turn a profit by just shopping there. I wanted to make sure that every person that reads this book would, at the very least, see thrifts in a different way. When you're driving by a sign that reads 'Thrift Store', I hope you have the urge to peek in and see what surprises await inside. As I talked to more and more people, I realized that there were very few individuals that actually realized how lucrative they could be. A lot of my friends used to see thrifts as a place full of unwanted things, items that would be better off in the trash. Even business-savvy people ignore the monetary potential that sits there patiently as they drive past it every morning to work. I wanted to change people's perspectives on these stores and make sure that they understand the importance of that random shop on their street corner.

Secondly, I wanted to give people a learning base in which to build their own thrift resell business. When I started my page, I knew just about nothing when it came to business tactics, marketing, or analysis. It took me years to finally learn the ins and outs of the thrifts, money management, and business itself. I wanted to turn my struggles and years of learning into something beneficial that other people can use to skip the learning curve. Although business can often be the boring side to the resell game, it's still a necessary component to turning random items into cash. Some of us love the hunt of thrifting but don't know a thing about profitably selling the items, so I wanted to help people turn their hobby into a fun way to make some cash.

Finally, I wanted to make something both entertaining and educational. I'm the type of person that likes to have fun when I learn. Who doesn't? There are far too many boring ways to learn things, so I wanted to make it short and sweet. There's no point in adding unnecessary information just to make a book longer; I wanted to add everything that I found important while letting your imagination make up the rest for you. Thrifting is a personal journey, and it's an experience where you're supposed to have fun. If you have an idea that differs from what the book says, give it a shot! You might as well, all you've got to lose is a couple dollars on stuff that you had fun hunting for. At the end of the day, it's all about having fun and making some money while doing it.

I hope you have the adventure of a lifetime, and happy thrifting!

—

—

Acknowledgements

Although this book's existence was basically unknown until it's completion, I have people to thank. Firstly, big thanks to Mom, Dad, Kate, and Ryan. You guys have only complained slightly about me bringing in dozens of random items into the house every week, and I am eternally thankful every day that I have you in my life. I'd also like to thank my friends, both from thrifts and from other expenditures in my life. You all have given me the confidence to write this book and I composed this with you all in mind. I hope you all like it!

Much Love,
Patrick Spychalski

Made in the USA
Columbia, SC
27 December 2019